W9-ARM-615

Reading/Writing Companion

Mc
Graw
Hill

mheducation.com/prek-12

Copyright © 2023 McGraw Hill

All rights reserved. No part of this publication may be
reproduced or distributed in any form or by any means,
or stored in a database or retrieval system, without the
prior written consent of McGraw Hill, including, but not
limited to, network storage or transmission, or broadcast
for distance learning.

Send all inquiries to:
McGraw Hill
1325 Avenue of the Americas
New York, NY 10019

ISBN: 978-1-26-574080-1
MHID: 1-26-574080-1

Printed in the United States of America.

5 6 7 8 9 LMN 26 25 24 23 22

A

Welcome to
WONDERS!

We're here to help you set goals to build on the amazing things you already know. We'll also help you reflect on everything you'll learn.

Let's start by taking a look at the incredible things you'll do this year.

You'll build knowledge on exciting topics and find answers to interesting questions.

You'll read fascinating fiction, informational texts, and poetry and respond to what you read with your own thoughts and ideas.

And you'll research and write stories, poems, and essays of your own!

Here's a sneak peek at how you'll do it all.

"Let's go!"

You'll explore new ideas by reading groups of different texts about the same topic. These groups of texts are called *text sets*.

At the beginning of a text set, we'll help you set goals on the My Goals page. You'll see a bar with four boxes beneath each goal. Think about what you already know to fill in the bar. Here's an example.

I can read and understand realistic fiction.

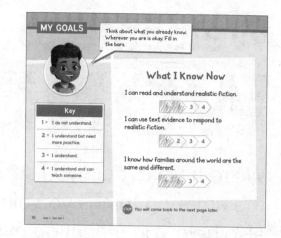

As you move through a text set, you'll explore an essential question and build your knowledge of a topic until you're ready to write about it yourself.

You'll also learn skills that will help you reach your text set goals. At the end of lessons, you'll see a new Check In bar with four boxes.

CHECK IN 1 2 3 4

Reflect on how well you understood a lesson to fill in the bar.

Here are some questions you can ask yourself.

- Was I able to complete the task?

- Was it easy or was it hard?

- Do I think I need more practice?

At the end of each text set, you'll show off the knowledge you built by completing a fun task. Then you'll return to the second My Goals page where we'll help you reflect on all that you learned.

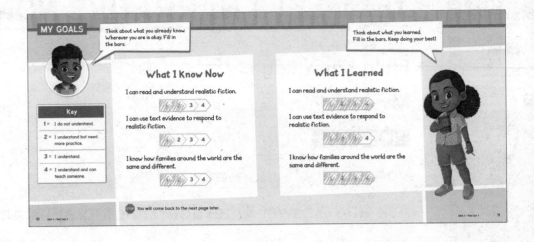

I'll fill in a new set of bars to show how far I've come. I started at 2, but now I'm at 4 because I can read and understand realistic fiction well enough to teach a friend.

I'll follow the same steps as I write my own stories, essays, and poems. I own my learning and you can own yours!

"Let's get started!"

TEXT SET 1 **NARRATIVE NONFICTION**

SOCIAL STUDIES

Alison Wright/Corbis Documentary/Getty Images

TEXT SET 2 **FICTION**

TEXT SET 3 **EXPOSITORY TEXT**

UNIT 3

EXTENDED WRITING

CONNECT AND REFLECT

jianying yin/Getty Images

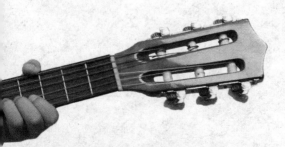

 Digital Tools

Find this eBook and other resources at **my.mheducation.com.**

Build Knowledge

Build Vocabulary

Write new words you learned about people helping their community. Draw lines and circles for the words you write.

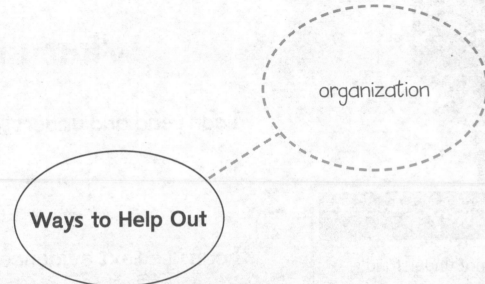

organization

Ways to Help Out

Go online to **my.mheducation.com** and read the "Making Our Lives Better ... Together" Blast. Think about how people work together to make their community a better place. Then blast back your response.

Superstudio/The Image Bank/Getty Images

Think about what you already know. Fill in the bars. This will be a good start.

Key

1 = I do not understand.

2 = I understand but need more practice.

3 = I understand.

4 = I understand and can teach someone.

What I Know Now

I can read and understand narrative nonfiction.

1 > 2 > 3 > 4

I can use text evidence to respond to narrative nonfiction.

1 > 2 > 3 > 4

I know about how people can help out their community.

1 > 2 > 3 > 4

 **STOP** You will come back to the next page later.

> Think about what you learned. Fill in the bars. What are you getting better at?

What I Learned

I can read and understand narrative nonfiction.

1 > 2 > 3 > 4

I can use text evidence to respond to narrative nonfiction.

1 > 2 > 3 > 4

I know about how people can help out their community.

1 > 2 > 3 > 4

My Goal I can read and understand narrative nonfiction.

TAKE NOTES

As you read, write down interesting words and important information.

_____

_____

_____

_____

_____

_____

_____

_____

Lighting Lives

Essential Question

? How can people help out their community?

Read to learn how one person is helping people in her community.

When Debby Tewa was your age, her home had no electricity. She could not flip a light switch to read at night. She lit a candle. She could not cook on a stove or in a microwave oven. Her family cooked over a fire.

Debby lived in Arizona. When she was ten, she moved to a new home. Her new home had electricity! She could turn on a lamp and use a phone. She liked it!

Debby Tewa lived in a home that had small windows like this one. There was not a lot of light.

FIND TEXT EVIDENCE

Read

Paragraph 1

Author's Purpose

Underline what the author explains about Debby's home at your age. **Circle** how she read at night and how her family cooked.

Paragraph 2

Combine Information

How did Debby's life change when she was ten?

_____

_____

_____

Reread

Author's Craft

How does the author help you understand what Debby's home was like when she was your age?

FIND TEXT EVIDENCE 🔍

Read

Paragraph 1

Author's Purpose

Underline details that explain the way people use solar panels.

Paragraph 2

Ask and Answer Questions

Ask a question about where Debby went to work. Write it below.

_____

_____

_____

Circle text evidence that helps you to answer it.

Reread

Author's Craft

How does the author use punctuation to show when Debby was excited?

As she grew, Debby realized she wanted to learn more about solar power. Solar power is electricity that comes from the Sun. Solar panels are put on the roof of a building. The sunlight hits these panels and turns into electricity.

Debby thought a lot about solar power. Then she had an **idea**! She was excited. She went to work for a company that provided solar power to people's homes. She believed it would be a good **solution** for people who had no electricity. Debby likes solving problems!

(t) Debby Tewa; (b) Bernhard Lang/Photographer's Choice/Getty Images.

Solar panels are now used on many homes.

Debby also thought of people in **villages** like the one she lived in as a child. The people in these small towns did not have any electricity. Solar power would work well there because there is a lot of sun in Arizona. Debby decided to help these families get solar power.

To get a family started, Debby helps them **borrow** money from a bank to buy the panels. After they get the money from the bank, they have some time to pay the money back. And the good news is there is no cost for using the Sun's power!

(t)Ellen McKnight/Alamy Stock Photo

NARRATIVE NONFICTION

FIND TEXT EVIDENCE

Read

Paragraph 1
Synonyms
Circle a word with almost the same meaning as *villages*. What did Debby decide to do for families in places without electricity?

_____

_____

_____

Author's Purpose
Underline the sentence that explains how Debby helps a family buy panels.

Reread
Author's Craft

How does the author help you understand why solar energy is a good solution for people Debby helps?

FIND TEXT EVIDENCE 🔍

`Read`

Paragraph 1

Photos and Captions

Draw a box around information that tells about the photograph.

What does Debby do when she travels to the countryside?

_____

_____

_____

Paragraph 2

Ask and Answer Questions
Underline text evidence that answers the question: _How does Debby help Hopi children?_

Debby travels **across** lands outside cities in Arizona and New Mexico. She travels to the **countryside**. She helps Hopi and Navajo people get solar power.

Debby believes deeply in her work and **insists** that families learn about how solar power can help them. They are happy to do what she demands. Debby also travels to schools and summer camps to teach Hopi children about solar energy.

Debby helps many Hopi people.

(bkgd) Luc Novovitch/Alamy Stock Photo; (l) Alison Wright/Corbis Documentary/Getty Images

Debby drives her truck from place to place. It is **lonely** with no one riding along. Then she thinks about how exciting it was to use electricity for the first time. Now families can do the things you do without thinking about them. They can heat their homes or turn on a light! Debby says she is "lighting up people's lives."

Retell

Use your notes and think about how Debby helps her community get electricity in "Lighting Lives." Retell the text using important details.

FIND TEXT EVIDENCE

Read

Author's Purpose
Circle the description of what it is like when Debby drives from place to place. **Underline** what Debby thinks about.

Reread

Author's Craft

What does Debby mean when she says she is "lighting up people's lives"? Why does the author include this quote?

Vocabulary

Use the sentences to talk with a partner about each word. Then answer the questions.

across

We walked **across** the street.

What are other things you can walk across?

_____

_____

borrow

I like to **borrow** books from the library.

What can you borrow from a friend?

_____

_____

> **Build Your Word List** Choose a word that you noted while reading. Use a print or digital thesaurus to look up synonyms for the word. Use one pair of synonyms in your own sentences.

countryside

The **countryside** is full of grass and trees.

What else may be in the countryside?

_____

_____

idea

Kate has an **idea** for the class project.

Name an idea you have for a game to play.

_____

_____

insists

Mom **insists** we wear our seatbelts.

What is something your teacher insists that you and your classmates do?

_____

_____

lonely

The boy was **lonely** when his friend moved away.

When have you felt lonely?

_____

_____

solution

Dylan found a **solution** for his problem.

What is a solution for spilled milk?

_____

_____

villages

Few people live in the small **villages** on the mountain.

What would it be like to visit a small village?

_____

_____

Synonyms

Synonyms are words that have almost the same meaning such as *big* and *large*.

FIND TEXT EVIDENCE

I read how Debby "insists" families learn about solar power and that they do what she "demands." I can tell insists *and* demands *are synonyms here. Both words mean "asks in a strong way" in the text.*

Debby believes deeply in her work and insists that families learn about how solar power can help them. They are happy to do what she demands.

Your Turn Think of a synonym for these words in "Lighting Lives."

home, page 13 _____

power, page 15 _____

CHECK IN 1 2 3 4

Alison Wright/Corbis Documentary/Getty Images

Ask and Answer Questions

Asking yourself questions helps you think about information in the selection. You can ask yourself questions before, during, and after you read.

🔍 **FIND TEXT EVIDENCE**

As I read page 14 of "Lighting Lives," I ask myself "What is solar power?" I will reread and look at the photos to find the answer to this question.

Quick Tip

Stop and ask yourself questions about difficult information that you have read or heard. Then reread to find the answers to your questions.

Page 14

As she grew, Debby realized she wanted to learn more about solar power. Solar power is electricity that comes from the Sun. Solar panels are put on the roof of a building. The sunlight hits these panels and turns into electricity.

I read that solar power is electricity that comes from the Sun. From this, I understand that solar panels use energy from the Sun.

Your Turn Write a question about how solar power can help people. Reread the parts of the selection that help you to answer it.

_____

_____

CHECK IN ▷ 1 ▷ 2 ▷ 3 ▷ 4 ▷

Photographs and Captions

"Lighting Lives" is narrative nonfiction. It tells a true story about a person by a narrator. It can have text features, such as photographs and captions.

Quick Tip

Pay close attention to photographs and captions. Authors often use them to help you understand important details about the topic.

🔍 **FIND TEXT EVIDENCE**

I can use what I read to tell that "Lighting Lives" is narrative nonfiction. A narrator tells about a real person, Debby Tewa.

Page 16

Debby travels **across** lands outside cities in Arizona and New Mexico. She travels to the **countryside**. She helps Hopi and Navajo people get solar power.

Debby believes deeply in her work and **insists** that families learn about how solar power can help them. They are happy to do what she demands. Debby also travels to schools and summer camps to teach Hopi children about solar energy.

Debby helps many Hopi people.

Photographs

A photograph shows something in the text or gives more information about a topic.

Captions

A caption gives details about a photo.

Your Turn How do the photographs and caption on pages 14 and 15 help you understand how solar panels are used?

_____

_____

CHECK IN 1 2 3 4

Author's Purpose

An author has a purpose, or reason, for writing. An author writes narrative nonfiction to inform, or teach, readers about a topic.

🔍 **FIND TEXT EVIDENCE**

When I read page 14 of "Lighting Lives," I learned how Debby Tewa got the idea to help others. I think this is a clue to the author's purpose.

> **Clue**
>
> Author tells how Debby Tewa got the idea to help people who did not have electricity in their homes.

Your Turn Continue reading the selection. Fill in a clue and the author's purpose on the graphic organizer.

Debby Tewa

CHECK IN ⟩ 1 ⟩ 2 ⟩ 3 ⟩ 4

Clue

Author tells how Debby Tewa got the idea to help people who did not have electricity in their homes.

Clue

Author's Purpose

Respond to Reading

Talk about the prompt below. Use your notes and text evidence to support your response.

How is Debby Tewa "lighting up people's lives"?

_____

_____

_____

_____

_____

_____

_____

_____

Quick Tip

Use these sentence starters to help you organize your text evidence.

When Debby was little,...

Debby had an idea...

People can now use...

Grammar Connections

Remember that a present-tense verb must agree with its subject.

*The children **learn** about solar power.*

*Debby **helps** people.*

*People **buy** solar panels.*

CHECK IN 1 2 3 4

History Picture Book

COLLABORATE

With a partner, create a picture book about an important person in the history of your town or state. Follow the research process to create your book.

Step 1 **Set a Goal** Discuss why the person is important and what you want to find out more about.

Write your topic: _____

Step 2 **Identify Sources** Use primary sources or secondary sources to find information. Primary sources come from people's lives. Letters and photographs may be primary sources. Secondary sources are written by people who studied a topic.

Step 3 **Find and Record Information** Take notes from the sources in your own words. Cite both the primary and secondary sources you used.

Step 4 **Organize and Combine Information** Put events and facts in the order they happened. Summarize in your own words why the person was important.

Step 5 **Create and Present** Add pictures and captions. Take turns presenting to your class the most important information illustrated in your book.

Quick Tip

In a primary source, a person describes or shows an event that he or she was at or took part in. The person may use *I* or *we* when describing what happened.

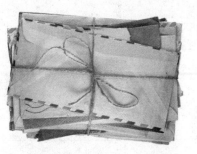

windujedi/iStock/Getty Images

Letters can tell us about important people and events from long ago.

CHECK IN 1 2 3 4

Biblioburro

 How does the author help you understand Luis's idea?

Literature Anthology: pages 212–233

Talk About It Reread page 215. Discuss what Luis pictured in his head as he was thinking.

Text Evidence Complete the chart with details from the illustration and text that show Luis's idea.

Quick Tip

"Biblioteca" is the Spanish word for "library" and "burro" is the Spanish word for "donkey." *Biblioburro* is a combination of the two words.

Illustration	Text

Write The author helps me understand _____

_____

_____

CHECK IN 1 > 2 > 3 > 4 >

How does the author help you understand what it was like to travel to the villages?

Talk About It Reread pages 220–221. Describe what you see in the illustration.

Cite Text Evidence Write three details you see in the illustration and make an inference about Luis's travels.

I see	I see	I see

Traveling to the villages was...

Write The author helps me understand that _____

_____

_____

Quick Tip

Use these sentence starters to talk about the illustration.

I see...

This makes me think...

Combine Information

Look back at pages 218–219. What words does the author use to describe the villages and hills where Luis traveled every week?

CHECK IN 1 2 3 4

? **What clues does the author use to show you how the children felt about the books?**

COLLABORATE

Talk About It Reread pages 226–227. Talk about what the children were doing and how they felt.

Cite Text Evidence Complete the chart with clues from the text and illustration.

Quick Tip

The author uses illustrations to help show how the children felt about books and reading.

The children were...   **The children felt...**

Write I know how the children felt about the books

because _____

_____

_____

CHECK IN ⟩ 1 ⟩ 2 ⟩ 3 ⟩ 4 ⟩

D. Hurst/Alamy

Respond to Reading

COLLABORATE Discuss the prompt below. Use your notes and text evidence to support your response.

Why is it important for Luis to travel to faraway villages each week?

_____

_____

_____

_____

_____

_____

_____

Quick Tip

Use these sentence starters to organize your text evidence.

Luis loves...
Luis and the burros bring...
The children of the village...
At night, Luis...

CHECK IN ▶ 1 ⟩ 2 ⟩ 3 ⟩ 4 ⟩

Landing on Your Feet

Before I wake up for school, Dad is already at work. He is an ironworker in the city. Ironworkers build tall buildings and repair giant bridges. They build with heavy metal beams made of iron. When Dad comes home, he likes to cook or do things for our house. He also teaches his favorite sport to kids. Dad is a gymnastics coach at a community center. He teaches girls like me at the same gym where he learned gymnastics as a boy.

Gymnastics is fun but hard to learn. Dad encourages us to practice to get better.

Literature Anthology: pages 234–237

Reread the text. **Underline** details that describe the narrator's dad.

What details help you understand the narrator is a young girl?

_____

_____

_____

_____

COLLABORATE

Discuss why the narrator begins her personal narrative with details about her dad and gymnastics.

(Colored pencils)Tatiana Popova/Shutterstock

The ice pack seemed to help Dad relax on the couch. I got pillows so he could put his leg up. Dad said, "I hope my ankle gets better soon. I need to coach the kids on Monday." Now I was really worried. Dad is always there for the kids at the gym. *I have until Monday to help Dad feel better,* I thought.

Reread the text. **Underline** details that show Ryan is concerned about her dad.

Circle details that show Ryan was concerned about the kids at the gym. Why does she have until Monday to help Dad feel better?

_____

_____

_____

COLLABORATE

Discuss Ryan's feelings and thoughts in the text and why she includes these details.

Olha Ukhal/Shutterstock

? **Why did the author write "Landing on Your Feet"?**

COLLABORATE

Talk About It Reread pages 234–237 of the **Literature Anthology.** Discuss the important events in Ryan's story.

Cite Text Evidence Fill in the chart with what Ryan describes took place Friday, over the weekend, and Monday.

Friday	Over the Weekend	Monday

The author wrote her personal narrative _____

_____

_____

Quick Tip

To help you understand and remember important details, paraphrase events in the order they happen in the story. To paraphrase is to use your own words to tell about what happens.

CHECK IN 1 2 3 4

Author's Purpose

Quick Tip

Ryan uses time words such as "last night," "over the weekend," and "after practice" to help you understand when each event in her personal narrative happened.

In a personal narrative, the author's purpose is to inform the reader about experiences. Some authors use time words to help readers understand when events take place.

 FIND TEXT EVIDENCE
Draw a box around the time words that tell when Ryan was building a toy house. **Circle** the words that tell when she and her mom knew something was wrong.

> One Friday, I had free time after school. I was building a toy house for my toy cat. When Dad came home from work, Mom and I knew something was wrong.

 **Your Turn** Reread the last paragraph on page 236. Identify the time words the author, Ryan, uses. What do these time words help you understand?

_____

_____

_____

CHECK IN 1 > 2 > 3 > 4

? **What have you learned about the ways people help others from the selections and the poem?**

COLLABORATE

Talk About It Talk with a partner about how Mouse helps the Lion.

Cite Text Evidence **Underline** clues that show what the author thinks about the Mouse helping.

Write The selections I read and this poem help me understand how

_____

_____

_____

_____

_____

_____

_____

Quick Tip

Compare the selections using these sentence starters.

Luis wanted to...

Ryan's dad helped their community by...

The Mouse is able to...

The Mouse and the Lion

A poor thing the Mouse was, and yet
When the Lion got caught in a net,
All his strength was no use
'Twas the poor little Mouse
Who nibbled him out of the net.
SMALL CAUSES MAY PRODUCE GREAT RESULTS

– Walter Crane

CHECK IN ▷ 1 ⟩ 2 ⟩ 3 ⟩ 4 ⟩

My Goal I know about how people can help out their community.

Write an Article

Think about the ways people help others in the texts you read. Think about the challenges they face. What motivates them, or makes them want, to help people in their communities?

1. Look at your Build Knowledge notes in your reader's notebook.

2. Write an article that could be published in a school newspaper or a magazine for kids. Report on three people you learned about. In your article, celebrate the work that these people do.

3. Include some of the new words you learned. Remember to use examples and evidence from the texts you read.

Think about what you learned in this text set. Fill in the bars on page 11.

Build Knowledge

Essential Question

What can we see in the sky?

Build Vocabulary

Write new words you learned about what we can see in the sky. Draw lines and circles for the words you write.

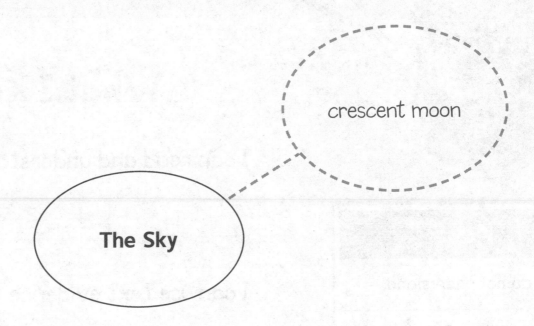

crescent moon

The Sky

Go online to **my.mheducation.com** and read the "When the Night Sky Dances" Blast. Think about how to see the Northern Lights. Then blast back your response.

ImagesBazaar/Vetta/Getty Images

Think about what you already know. Fill in the bars. It's okay if you want more practice.

Key
1 = I do not understand.
2 = I understand but need more practice.
3 = I understand.
4 = I understand and can teach someone.

What I Know Now

I can read and understand fiction.

1 > 2 > 3 > 4

I can use text evidence to respond to fiction.

1 > 2 > 3 > 4

I know about what we can see in the sky.

1 > 2 > 3 > 4

STOP You will come back to the next page later.

Think about what you learned. Fill in the bars. What progress did you make?

What I Learned

I can read and understand fiction.

1 2 3 4

I can use text evidence to respond to fiction.

1 2 3 4

I know about what we can see in the sky.

1 2 3 4

My Goal

I can read and understand fiction.

TAKE NOTES

As you read, write down interesting words and important events.

Starry Night

Essential Question

What can we see in the sky?

Read about what two girls learn when they look at the nighttime sky.

Josie and Ling were good friends. Ling was happy Josie was her **neighbor**. Josie was happy Ling lived nearby, too.

Josie and Ling couldn't wait for the school day to end. They planned a sleepover at Josie's house. They were going to sleep in a tent in Josie's backyard.

As the class was leaving, Mr. Cortes said, "Your weekend homework is to look at the **nighttime** sky and explain what you saw on Monday." The class **grumbled**. "Why the unhappy sounds?" Mr. Cortes asked. "It will be fun looking at the sky at night."

Chris Conga

FIND TEXT EVIDENCE 🔍

Read

Paragraphs 1–2
Character Perspective

Circle how the girls feel about being neighbors.
Underline why they cannot wait for school to end.

Paragraph 3
Reread

Draw a box around the weekend homework for the class. How does the class respond when they get homework?

_____

_____

Reread

Author's Craft

How does the author show Mr. Cortes feels differently from the class about the homework?

FIND TEXT EVIDENCE

Read

Paragraph 1

Compound Words

Circle the two smaller words in *outdoors*. Why are the girls delighted to be sleeping outdoors?

_____

_____

Paragraph 2

Plot: Sequence of Events

Underline text evidence that shows how the girls feel about doing homework at the time.

Reread

Author's Craft

Why is the setting in Josie's backyard at night important to the story?

The girls arrived at Josie's house and were **delighted** to be sleeping outdoors. Josie said, "I'm so happy that we get to sleep in the tent. It will be lots of fun." Then Ling said, "I'll get the sleeping bags and flashlights. I brought flashlights so we can play games in the tent."

Josie's dad poked his head inside the tent. "Girls, it is a good time to do your homework now because it is getting dark," he said. "Awww," they both complained. "Dad," said Josie, "do we have to, now?"

"Yes, I already set up the telescope."

Ling said, "I hope this won't take too long." Josie looked up and spotted a crescent moon. "Did you know the moon's light comes from the Sun?" said Josie. "It's funny that it's called **moonlight**." "Yes," said Ling, who was still thinking about playing in the tent.

Josie's dad smiled at the girls and said, "See the stars in the sky? Those points of bright light can form shapes."

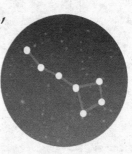

The Big Dipper

"You can see the Big Dipper," he said. "It's a group of stars that look like a giant spoon in the sky."

Chris Canga

FIND TEXT EVIDENCE

Read

Paragraph 1

Reread

Why does Josie say, "It's funny that it's called moonlight"? **Circle** details that support your answer.

_____

_____

_____

_____

Paragraph 2

Character Perspective

Underline the detail that shows Josie's dad likes helping the girls.

FIND TEXT EVIDENCE

Read

Paragraphs 2–3
Reread
Draw a box around what Ling cries out when she sees a shooting star.

Paragraphs 3–4
Plot: Sequence of Events
Underline what Ling says about looking at the stars. How do her feelings change after seeing the shooting star?

_____

_____

_____

Reread

Author's Craft

How does the author use Ling's dialogue to show her excitement?

Josie's dad showed her how to look through the telescope. "Wow, that's more stars than I ever **dreamed** of. I never imagined there could be so many."

It was Ling's turn to look. Ling cried out, "I see a bright light moving in the sky!"

"That's a shooting star!" said Josie's dad.

"This is fun," said Ling. "I really **enjoy** looking at the stars."

"I think we've seen enough of the nighttime sky," said Josie's dad. "You girls can go play now."

"Aw, Dad, can't we keep looking?" asked Josie. "This is really fun."

"Yes," said Ling. "We have had an **adventure** already, and we haven't even played in the tent yet!"

"You're right, Ling," said Josie. "This has been one exciting night."

Retell

Look at your notes and think about what happens in "Starry Night." Retell the story's events in the order they happen.

FIND TEXT EVIDENCE

Read

Paragraph 1
Plot: Sequence of Events
Circle what Josie's dad says the girls can do now.

Paragraphs 2–3
Reread
Underline what Josie asks her dad. What do the girls want to do?

_____

_____

_____

Reread

Author's Craft

How does the author show the girls feel differently about their homework assignment?

Vocabulary

Talk with a partner about each word. Then answer the questions.

adventure

It's an **adventure** to hike in the woods.

What kind of trip would be an adventure?

_____

_____

delighted

Lin is **delighted** to see her grandmother.

What makes you feel delighted?

_____

_____

📝 **Build Your Word List** Write a sentence using an interesting word you listed on page 40. Use a dictionary to help you.

dreamed

Juan **dreamed** about being an actor.

What is something you dreamed about?

_____

_____

enjoy

We **enjoy** playing in the pool in the summer.

What do you enjoy doing in the summer?

_____

_____

grumbled

My brother **grumbled** because Mom told him to clean his room.

Name something that makes you grumble.

_____

_____

moonlight

The **moonlight** is very bright when the Moon is full.

What can moonlight help you do at night?

_____

_____

neighbor

I went across the street to play with my **neighbor**.

Tell about a neighbor you know.

_____

_____

nighttime

At **nighttime** you can see stars in the sky.

What else can you see at nighttime?

_____

_____

Compound Words

A compound word is made up of two smaller words. The meanings of the smaller words can help you figure out the meaning of a compound word.

🔍 **FIND TEXT EVIDENCE**

The first part of sleepover *is* sleep, *which means "to close your eyes and rest." The second part is* over, *which can mean "at another place." I think* sleepover *means "sleeping at someone's house."*

They planned a sleepover at Josie's house.

Your Turn Use the smaller words to figure out the meaning of a compound word on page 41.

backyard _____

CHECK IN ▶ 1 ⟩ 2 ⟩ 3 ⟩ 4 ⟩

Chris Canga

Reread

As you read, stop and ask yourself questions about the text. If you can't answer them, reread the parts you do not understand or may have missed. This will help you understand what you read.

 **FIND TEXT EVIDENCE**

On page 43 of "Starry Night," I am not sure what the Big Dipper is. I will reread this part of the story to see if I missed anything.

Page 43

Josie's dad smiled at the girls and said, "See the stars in the sky? Those points of bright light can form shapes."

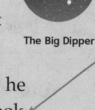

The Big Dipper

"You can see the Big Dipper," he said. "It's a group of stars that look like a giant spoon in the sky."

When I reread that the Big Dipper is a group of stars that look like a giant spoon in the sky and I look at the picture, I understand what the Big Dipper is.

 Your Turn What does Ling see when she looks through the telescope? Reread page 44 to answer the question.

Quick Tip

Pay attention to words that tell about actions and words that describe sensory details, such as how something looks or sounds.

CHECK IN 1 2 3 4

Character Perspective

"Starry Night" is a fiction story with made-up characters and events. Fiction stories can have a narrator that is not a character. It is called third-person point of view. The narrator can describe the perspectives of any character.

Quick Tip

Perspective is a character's attitude, or feeling, about something. Third-person point of view allows authors to describe how many characters feel.

 FIND TEXT EVIDENCE

I can tell that "Starry Night" is a made-up story that shows the perspectives of different characters.

Page 42

The girls arrived at Josie's house and were **delighted** to be sleeping outdoors. Josie said, "I'm so happy that we get to sleep in the tent. It will be lots of fun." Then Ling said, "I'll get the sleeping bags and flashlights. I brought flashlights so we can play games in the tent."

Josie's dad poked his head inside the tent. "Girls, it is a good time to do your homework now because it is getting dark," he said. "Awww," they both complained. "Dad," said Josie, "do we have to, now?"

"Yes, I already set up the telescope."

Character Perspective

The narrator describes the perspective, or attitude, of the girls. They are "delighted to be sleeping outdoors."

 Your Turn How are the perspectives of the girls different from Josie's dad's?

COLLABORATE

_____

_____

_____

CHECK IN 1 2 3 4

Plot: Sequence of Events

The sequence of events is the order that events happen in the story. We can use the words *first*, *next*, *then*, and *last* to tell the order of what happens.

🔍 FIND TEXT EVIDENCE

As I read page 41 of "Starry Night," I think about the sequence of the story.

| **First** |
| Josie and Ling plan a sleepover. |

↓

Your Turn Continue rereading "Starry Night." Fill in the graphic organizer to tell the sequence of events of the story.

COLLABORATE

Quick Tip

Authors often use signal words and phrases such as *at the beginning, later, before, in the meantime,* and *after* to show the order of events in a story.

CHECK IN 1 2 3 4

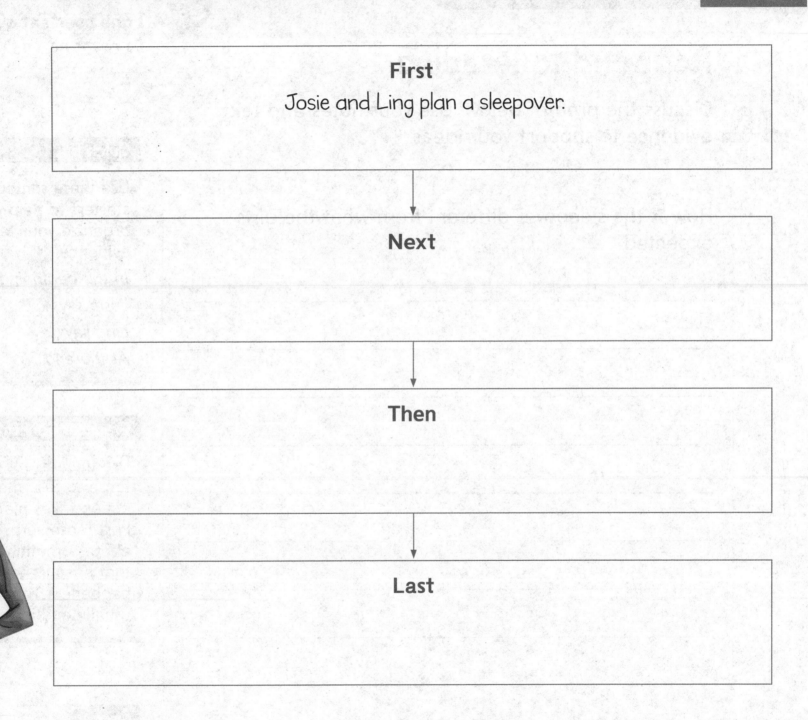

First

Josie and Ling plan a sleepover.

Next

Then

Last

My Goal

I can use text evidence to respond to fiction.

Respond to Reading

COLLABORATE

Discuss the prompt below. Use your notes and text evidence to support your ideas.

How is the sleepover different from what the girls expected?

_____

_____

_____

_____

_____

_____

_____

Quick Tip

Use these sentence starters to help you organize your text evidence.

In the beginning...

Josie says...

Ling says...

At the end...

Grammar Connections

Use the correct verb tense to tell when an action takes place. Past-tense verbs tell about something that has already happened. They usually end in -ed.

CHECK IN 1 2 3 4

Seasons

COLLABORATE

With a partner, follow the research process to write a report about the weather during a season in your state.

Step 1 **Set a Goal** Discuss the season you will report on. Talk about questions your report will answer.

Write your topic: _____

Step 2 **Identify Sources** Use relevant sources such as trusted websites to find information. Discuss keywords to use to find information.

Write keywords for your research: _____

_____

Think about questions you can ask about the weather in winter, spring, summer, and fall in your state.

Step 3 **Find and Record Information** Write down facts and the sources of this information. Summarize ideas you read about in your own words.

Step 4 **Organize and Combine Information** Group together details that support the main points about the topic.

Step 5 **Create and Present** Write and illustrate your report. Plan on how to present its main points and supporting details to the class.

CHECK IN ⟩ 1 ⟩ 2 ⟩ 3 ⟩ 4 ⟩

Mr. Putter & Tabby See the Stars

? **Why does Mrs. Teaberry like to feed Mr. Putter "most of all"?**

Literature Anthology: pages 238–257

Talk About It Reread pages 242 and 243. Talk about how you know that the two characters like each other.

Cite Text Evidence Write clues from the text that tell you Mrs. Teaberry likes Mr. Putter more than other people.

Make Inferences

What do you understand about Mrs. Teaberry and Mr. Putter when they lose track of time while being together?

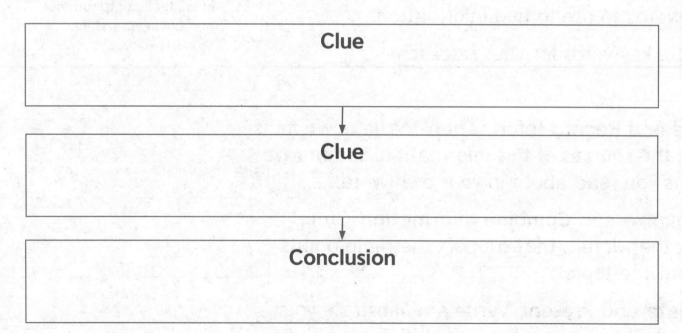

Clue

↓

Clue

↓

Conclusion

Write Mrs. Teaberry likes to feed Mr. Putter the most

because _____

CHECK IN 1 2 3 4

How do you know that Mrs. Teaberry and Mr. Putter are becoming better friends?

Talk About It Reread page 253. Talk about what Mrs. Teaberry and Mr. Putter are doing.

Cite Text Evidence Write clues that tell that Mrs. Teaberry and Mr. Putter are becoming better friends.

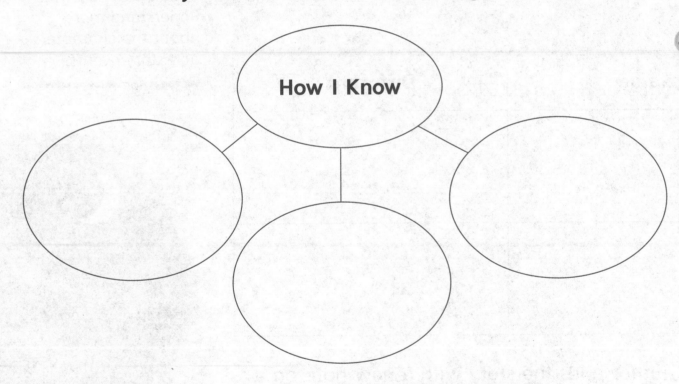

How I Know

Quick Tip

As you read, use these sentence starters to talk about what friends do.

The characters are...
This helps me see...

Combine Information

Use details you already know about Mr. Putter and Mrs. Teaberry to build on your understanding of their friendship.

Write I know that Mrs. Teaberry and Mr. Putter are

becoming better friends because _____

_____

CHECK IN 1 2 3 4

? **Why does the author end the story with a new note on a new day?**

Talk About It Look at the illustration on page 255. Discuss with a partner what Mr. Putter is holding and why.

Cite Text Evidence Write clues that show how the next morning might be the same and how it might be different.

COLLABORATE

Quick Tip

Look closely at story illustrations. Sometimes there are details in the pictures that aren't in the text. These details can help you understand more about the characters and story events.

Same	Different

Write The author ends the story with a new note on a new day to _____

_____

CHECK IN   1   2   3   4

Respond to Reading

COLLABORATE

Discuss the prompt below. Use your notes and text evidence to support your response.

How does the friendship between Mr. Putter and Mrs. Teaberry change one night?

_____

_____

_____

_____

_____

_____

_____

_____

Quick Tip

Use these sentence starters to organize your text evidence.

One night, Mr. Putter eats...

Mrs. Teaberry and Zeke...

Mr. Putter and Mrs. Teaberry talk...

In the morning,...

CHECK IN 1 2 3 4

Day to Night

Literature Anthology:
pages 258-261

Your alarm clock rings. *Beep! Beep! Beep!* You turn it off, stretch, and get out of bed. You look out the window and see the daytime sky.

The Daytime Sky

The sky is light today. It is blue with white clouds and the bright Sun. The Sun is the brightest object in the sky. It looks small, but that is because it is far from Earth.

Sometimes the daytime sky has clouds.

Marc Romanelli/The Image Bank/Getty Images

Reread paragraph 1. How does the author grab your attention at the beginning? **Draw a box** around the evidence. Why does the author start the selection that way?

_____

_____

_____

Reread paragraph 2. **Underline** a sentence that tells what the daytime sky looks like.

COLLABORATE

Circle the title. Talk with a partner about whether it is a good one. Then choose a new title for the selection together.

The Nighttime Sky

At the end of the day, you look out the window before you get into bed. The sky is dark. It is nighttime. Tonight you see part of the Moon. Without the bright light from the Sun, you are able to see light from many stars.

The stars look like tiny points of light, but each one is very big.

Reread the paragraph. **Underline** details about the two major differences between the daytime sky and the nighttime sky. Write them here.

_____

_____

_____

COLLABORATE

Talk about what you learn about the night sky from the photograph.

Russell Kord/Alamy Stock Photo

? **Why did the author write "Day to Night"?**

Talk About It Reread pages 258–261. Talk with a partner about what you learned from "Day to Night."

Cite Text Evidence Write facts you learned from the text. Then write why the author wrote "Day to Night."

Fact	Fact	Fact

The author wrote this to...

Write The author wrote "Day to Night" to _____

_____

_____

Quick Tip

"Day to Night" is an expository text. Authors write expository texts to inform readers. To figure out what an author is trying to inform you about, ask yourself "What does the author want me to learn?"

CHECK IN 1 > 2 > 3 > 4 >

Headings

Expository texts often have headings that separate a text into parts. The headings are usually printed in big, bold type. Authors use them to tell you what the different sections of the text are about.

FIND TEXT EVIDENCE

Take another look at "Day to Night." Write the headings on the lines below.

_____   _____

_____   _____

_____

Your Turn Look back at the headings in "Day to Night" one more time. Why do you think some are orange and some are blue?

_____

_____

_____

Quick Tip

A heading is like the title of a section in the text. Sometimes a heading gives you a clue about the most important ideas in the section. When you want to find certain information in a text, you can use the headings to help guide you.

CHECK IN 1 2 3 4

? How do the selections you read and the painting help you understand how the sky changes from day to night?

Talk About It Talk about what you see in the sky in the painting. Talk about what people see in the sky as it changes from day to night.

Cite Text Evidence **Circle** a clue in the caption that tells you what time of day it is in the painting.

Write The selections and the painting show

_____

_____

_____

_____

_____

_____

_____

William Turner of Oxford/Yale Center for British Art Paul Mellon Collection

Quick Tip

Describe the evening sky using these sentence starters:

In the daytime sky, I can see...

Without the bright light from the Sun, I can see...

This painting of an evening sky by William Turner shows daylight fading on the horizon and a comet in the sky.

CHECK IN 1 2 3 4

My Goal I know about what we can see in the sky.

Write an Invitation

Think about how people view the sky in the texts you read and what you have learned. Why do people study the Moon, stars, and planets? Write an invitation to a class astronomy club that studies outer space.

1. Look at your Build Knowledge notes in your reader's notebook.

2. Write to children the reasons to join a class astronomy club. Tell about the fascinating things the kids can learn together. Use examples from three texts. Show how learning about the nighttime sky is interesting and fun.

3. Include some of the new words you learned. Remember to use evidence from three texts to support your ideas.

Think about what you learned in this text set. Fill in the bars on page 39.

Build Knowledge

Essential Question
How do you express yourself?

Build Vocabulary

Write new words you learned about how we express ourselves. Draw lines and circles for the words you write.

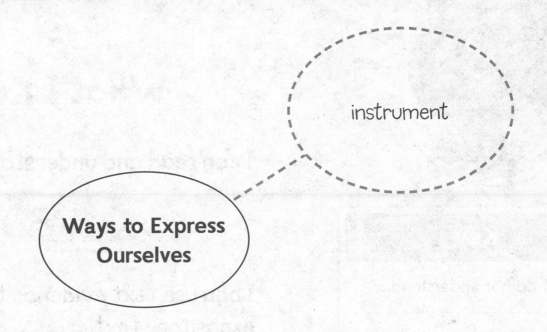

instrument

Ways to Express Ourselves

Go online to **my.mheducation.com** and read the "Show Yourself Through Art" Blast. Think about the ways art lets us express ourselves. Then blast back your response.

Unit 3 • Text Set 3   65

Think about what you already know. Fill in the bars. Let's keep learning!

What I Know Now

I can read and understand expository text.

1 > 2 > 3 > 4

I can use text evidence to respond to expository text.

1 > 2 > 3 > 4

I know about how we can express ourselves.

1 > 2 > 3 > 4

Key	
1 =	I do not understand.
2 =	I understand but need more practice.
3 =	I understand.
4 =	I understand and can teach someone.

STOP You will come back to the next page later.

Think about what you learned. Fill in the bars. Keep working hard!

What I Learned

I can read and understand expository text.

1 2 3 4

I can use text evidence to respond to expository text.

1 2 3 4

I know about how we can express ourselves.

1 2 3 4

My Goal I can read and understand expository text.

TAKE NOTES

As you read, write down interesting words and important information.

TIME for KiDS

Essential Question

? **How do you express yourself?**

Read about how children in a school chorus express themselves.

(l)Carrie Devorah/WENN.com/Newscom; (r)Christa Maniglia

They've Got the Beat!

Some students in New York really sing their hearts out! That's because they are in the school chorus at Public School 22.

These students from Staten Island had a **concert** at the White House. They sang at a Hollywood awards show. Audiences have clapped and **cheered** them on. These kids are always asked to return.

How does it feel to sing on stage? "I get nervous singing for a big audience," Brianna Crispino recalls. "But when I see the joy on their faces, I get excited."

Brianna Crispino,
Public School 22 Chorus Member

TEXT EVIDENCE

FIND TEXT EVIDENCE

Read

Paragraphs 1–2
Central Idea and Details
Circle words that describe where the chorus is from.
Draw a box around places where they traveled to sing.

Paragraph 3
Ask and Answer Questions
Think of a question about the feelings Brianna describes. Write it here.

_____

_____

Underline clues that help answer your question.

Reread

Author's Craft

How does the author grab your attention in the opening paragraph?

Sounds Good

Bebeto Matthews/AP Images

FIND TEXT EVIDENCE

Read

Paragraph 1

Central Idea and Details

Underline the definitions of the two groups of singers. Why do all the singers keep the rhythm?

Paragraph 2

Idioms

Circle the words the author uses to invite you to review the graph.

Reread

Author's Craft

How does the author compare the school chorus with most adult choruses?

The Public School 22 chorus is divided into two groups. The sopranos sing high notes. The altos sing lower **sounds**. **Instruments** like drums sometimes keep the beat. It's important to keep the **rhythm** so they make the right sounds together.

Most adult choruses have four groups of voices. Here's a look at the number of each type of voice in one adult chorus from Pennsylvania.

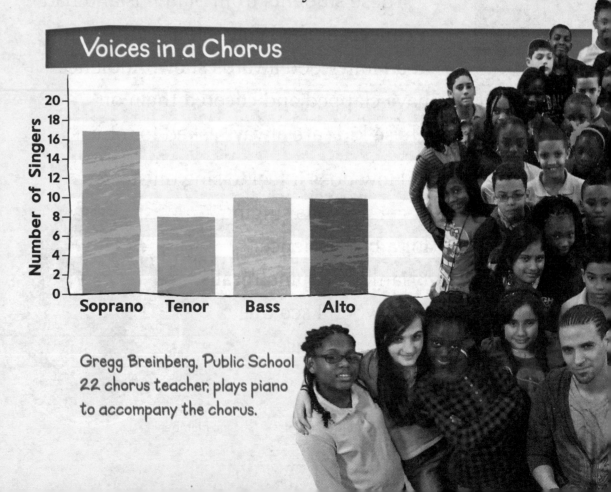

Voices in a Chorus

Number of Singers: 0, 2, 4, 6, 8, 10, 12, 14, 16, 18, 20

Soprano   Tenor   Bass   Alto

Gregg Breinberg, Public School 22 chorus teacher, plays piano to accompany the chorus.

Musical Expression

Being part of the chorus is hard work. The chorus members won't disagree. They practice for three hours each week.

Gregg Breinberg, their teacher, encourages the chorus to use **movements**. They move their hands to show how the songs make them feel. "They have their own movements because nobody feels **music** the same way," he explains.

The chorus members **understand** that singing in a chorus is a big job. "We just want to give it our best!" one student says.

Retell

Use your notes and think about the most important details in the text. Then retell "They've Got the Beat!"

TEXT EVIDENCE

FIND TEXT EVIDENCE

Read

Paragraph 1

Prefixes

The prefix *dis-* means "opposite of." **Circle** the word with the prefix *dis-*. Write the word's meaning.

_____

_____

Paragraph 2

Ask and Answer Questions

Why does Gregg Breinberg encourage the chorus to use movements? **Underline** text evidence to answer.

Reread

Author's Craft

How does the author use a student's comment to support ideas in the text?

Vocabulary

**Talk with a partner about each word.
Then answer the questions.**

cheered
We **cheered** for the runners in the race.

Who have you cheered for?

_____

_____

concert
Jack played the drums in the **concert**.

Tell about a concert you saw.

_____

_____

> **Build Your Word List** Choose an interesting word that you noted while reading. Look up its meaning in the dictionary. Write a sentence using the word in your reader's notebook.

instrument
A violin is a musical **instrument**.

What musical instruments can you name?

_____

_____

movements
The dancer's **movements** are exciting.

What movements do you make when you dance?

_____

_____

music
Dad's favorite kind of **music** is jazz.

What is your favorite kind of music?

_____

_____

rhythm

We clapped to the **rhythm** of the song.

What is another word for rhythm?

_____

_____

sounds

A flute can make soft **sounds**.

What can make really loud sounds?

_____

_____

understand

Ken did not **understand** the rules of the game.

What can you do when a paragraph is hard to understand?

_____

_____

Prefixes

A prefix is a word part at the beginning of a word. To figure out a word's meaning, separate the base word from its prefix.

🔍 **FIND TEXT EVIDENCE**

I'm not sure what return *means. I know* turn *means "to move around in a circle." The prefix* re- *means "again" or "back." Return* means "to come around again."

These kids are always asked to return .

Your Turn Use the prefix *re-* to help you understand a word from the selection. Write the definition.

recalls, page 69 _____

_____

CHECK IN ▷ 1 ▷ 2 ▷ 3 ▷ 4 ▷

Carrie Devorah/WENN.com/Newscom

Ask and Answer Questions

When you read, asking questions helps you think about important details of the text that you may have missed or do not understand.

🔍 FIND TEXT EVIDENCE

As I read page 71 of "They've Got the Beat!," I ask myself, "Why is singing in the chorus hard work?" I will reread to find the answer.

Quick Tip

As you read, think of questions you have about the text. You can reread the text to answer your questions, or keep your questions in mind as you continue to read.

Page 71

> Being part of the chorus is hard work. The chorus members won't disagree. They practice for three hours each week.

I reread that the chorus practices "three hours each week." This text evidence answers my question.

Your Turn Think of a question you have about the selection. Reread parts of the text to help you answer the question. Write your question and answer here.

_____

_____

CHECK IN 1 2 3 4

Figurative Language: Idioms

Quick Tip

Remember that an idiom is a group of words that together have a special meaning.

"They've Got the Beat!" is an expository text. It gives facts and information about a topic. It has text features and figurative language such as idioms.

🔍 FIND TEXT EVIDENCE

I know that "They've Got the Beat!" is an expository text. It presents information about a chorus. It has idioms that help me understand that the topic is about real kids.

Page 69

They've Got the Beat!

Some students in New York really sing their hearts out! That's because they are in the school chorus at Public School 22.

These students from Staten Island had a **concert** at the White House. They sang at a Hollywood awards show. Audiences have clapped and **cheered** them on. These kids are always asked to return.

How does it feel to sing on stage? "I get nervous singing for a big audience," Brianna Crispino recalls. "But when I see the joy on their faces, I get excited."

Brianna Crispino, Public School 22 Chorus Member

Idioms
Idioms such as "sing their hearts out" show how the kids really feel about being in a chorus.

 Your Turn What do the idioms *a big job* and *give it our best* mean on page 71?

COLLABORATE

_____

_____

_____

CHECK IN ⟩ 1 ⟩ 2 ⟩ 3 ⟩ 4 ⟩

Central Idea and Relevant Details

Quick Tip

Think about what
the details have in
common, or what
they all tell about.
This will help you
to identify the
central idea.

The central idea is the most important point an author
makes about a topic. Relevant details tell about and
support the central idea.

 FIND TEXT EVIDENCE

*As I read page 69 of "They've Got the Beat!," I
understand a relevant detail about the chorus is that
they performed at special places like the White House.*

> **Detail**
>
> They performed at
> the White House.

 Your Turn Continue rereading the selection. List
the relevant details and the central idea in the
graphic organizer.

CHECK IN 1 2 3 4

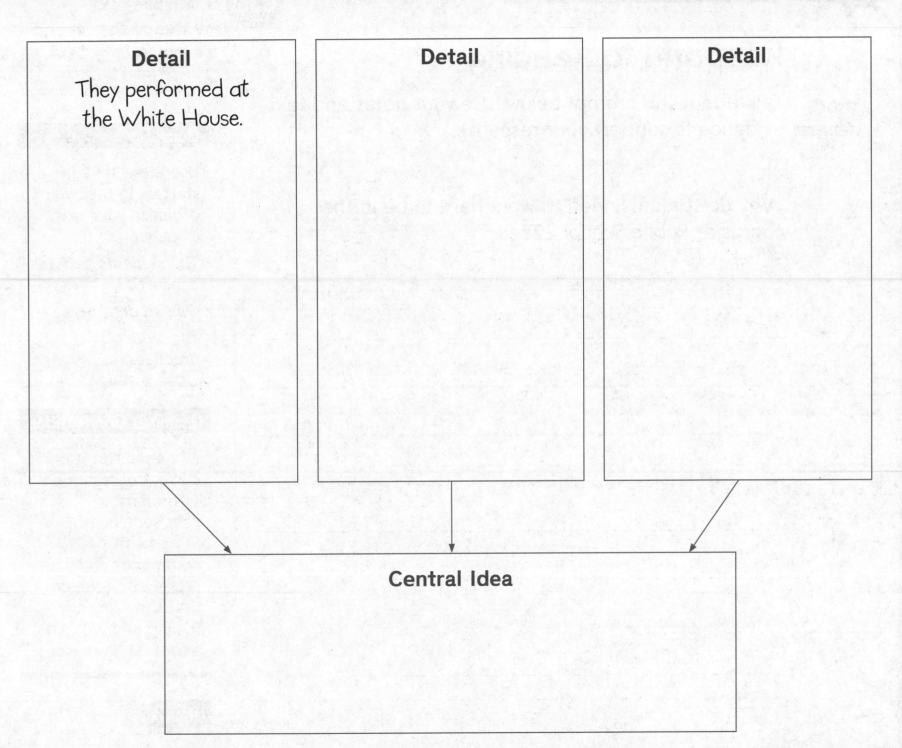

Detail

They performed at the White House.

Detail

Detail

Central Idea

Respond to Reading

Talk about the prompt below. Use your notes and text evidence to support your response.

Why do students need to work hard to be in the chorus at Public School 22?

_____

_____

_____

_____

_____

_____

_____

Quick Tip

Use these sentence starters to help you organize your text evidence.

The students had a concert at...

One student says...

The students practice...

Grammar Connections

Remember to use correct punctuation at the end of your sentences. Statements or commands end with a period. Sentences that show strong feeling end with an exclamation mark.

CHECK IN 1 2 3 4

National Symbols

With a partner, create a collage that answers the research question: *How does a monument, building, or document show or express something special about America?* Follow the research process to create your collage.

Step 1 **Set a Goal** Decide on a topic together.

Write your topic: _____

Step 2 **Identify Sources** Relevant sources can be books, magazine articles, or websites. Strong sources will answer the research question.

Step 3 **Find and Record Information** Take notes in your own words on the facts and details that answer the research question. Cite each source you use.

Step 4 **Organize and Combine Information** Organize the information you found. Write sentences in your own words that summarize important ideas.

Step 5 **Create and Present** Create your collage, adding the sentences you wrote. Add labels that give more facts and details. Share your collage with the class.

SerrNovik/iStock/Getty Images

CHECK IN 〉 1 〉 2 〉 3 〉 4 〉

Many Ways to Enjoy Music

? How does the author help you sense the excitement of a concert?

Literature Anthology: pages 262–265

Talk About It Reread page 263. Discuss details that describe what may happen at a concert.

Text Evidence What words are used to describe the concert? Write the text evidence in the web.

Make Inferences

Remember that an inference is an idea you get based on clues in the text. Why does the author want you to sense the excitement of a concert?

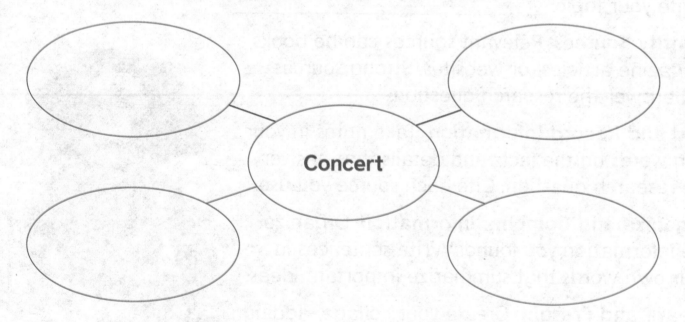

Concert

Write The author helps me sense the excitement of the concert _____

_____

CHECK IN 1 2 3 4

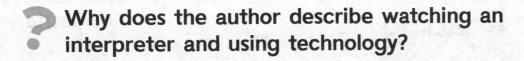

? **Why does the author describe watching an interpreter and using technology?**

Talk About It Look back at pages 264–265. Discuss the details about interpreters and the technology of a special chair.

Cite Text Evidence What details help you understand how music can be enjoyed in different ways? Write text evidence in the chart.

Quick Tip

Remember to read the captions to the photos. Often they can help you identify and understand important details that are in the text.

Interpreter	Special Chair

Write The author wants readers to understand how _____

_____

_____

CHECK IN ⟩ 1 ⟩ 2 ⟩ 3 ⟩ 4 ⟩

Respond to Reading

COLLABORATE

Discuss the prompt below. Use your notes and text evidence to support your response.

Why is "Many Ways to Enjoy Music" a good title for this selection?

_____

_____

_____

_____

_____

_____

_____

Quick Tip

Use these sentence starters to organize your response.

This is a good title because...

The author uses...

Another reason is...

A Musical Museum

Humans can hear almost every sound in nature. But some animals hear sounds you can't hear. Dogs and bats, for example, can hear very high sounds that don't reach human ears. What sounds do you like to listen to?

Sound is the energy things make when they move back and forth. Those back and forth movements are called vibrations.

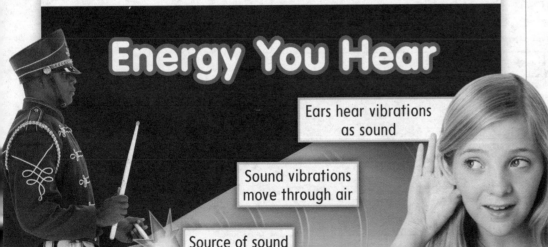

Energy You Hear

Ears hear vibrations as sound

Sound vibrations move through air

Source of sound vibrations

Literature Anthology: pages 266–267

Reread the text. **Underline** what humans can hear. **Draw a box** around the definition of sound.

Look back at the diagram. How do our ears hear vibrations?

_____

_____

COLLABORATE

Discuss how the diagram shows how a person can hear a drum.

(l)Ryan McVay/Stone/Getty Images;(r)Paul Hakimata/age fotostock

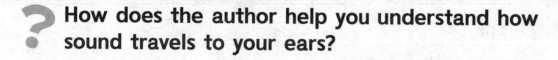

? **How does the author help you understand how sound travels to your ears?**

Talk About It Reread page 267 in the **Literature Anthology.** Discuss details that explain what sound is.

Cite Text Evidence Complete the chart. Write text evidence that explains how people hear sound.

COLLABORATE

> "Back and forth movements are called vibrations."

⬇

⬇

⬇

Write The author explains _____

_____

Quick Tip

In "A Musical Museum," the author explains how sound is created and travels to your ears. Pay attention to how each detail is connected. This will make the text easier to understand.

CHECK IN 1 2 3 4

Diagrams

A diagram is a graphic feature used in expository texts. Authors use diagrams to show the special parts of something or to explain how something works.

FIND TEXT EVIDENCE
Look back at the diagram on page 267. What three steps are shown in the diagram?

1. _____

2. _____

3. _____

Your Turn Reread the second paragraph. Discuss the information from the text shown in the diagram. What is an example of a text detail the author does not include in the diagram?

_____

_____

_____

Readers to Writers

Label each step in a diagram with a simple sentence or a phrase. Include only the most important information. You may number each step to show sequence, or the correct order of the information.

CHECK IN 1 2 3 4

MAKE CONNECTIONS

COLLABORATE

? What have you learned from the selections and the print from Japan about expressing yourself?

Talk About It Look at the print and read the caption. Talk with a partner about what the people are doing.

Cite Text Evidence **Underline** text evidence in the caption that tells what the artist shows. **Circle** two things the women are doing.

Write From the selections and the print, I have learned that

_____

_____

_____

_____

_____

_____

_____

BernardAllum/E+/Getty Images

This print from Japan, called an Ukiyo-e, shows a gathering of women playing a variety of musical instruments.

> **Quick Tip**
>
> Talk about how people enjoy music using these sentence starters.
>
> *A chorus moves...*
>
> *A concert is a place...*
>
> *People play music...*

CHECK IN 1 > 2 > 3 > 4 >

Plan a Video

Think about the ways people enjoy the arts, such as music, from the texts you read. Why should people explore the arts? Plan a video that shows how people can get involved in music or another kind of art.

1. Look at your Build Knowledge notes in your reader's notebook.

2. Choose three topics that interest you most from the texts you read. Write about the places, people, or performances. Plan to educate, or show, the audience how they can be involved in art too.

3. Include some of the new words you learned. Remember to use evidence from three of the texts to support your ideas.

Think about what you learned in this text set. Fill in the bars on page 67.

Think about what you already know. Fill in the bars. It's important to keep learning.

Key
1 = I do not understand.
2 = I understand but need more practice.
3 = I understand.
4 = I understand and can teach someone.

What I Know Now

I can write a personal narrative.

1 > 2 > 3 > 4 >

I can write an expository essay.

1 > 2 > 3 > 4 >

STOP You will come back to the next page later.

> Think about what you learned. Fill in the bars. What helped you do your best?

What I Learned

I can write a personal narrative.

1 > 2 > 3 > 4

I can write an expository essay.

1 > 2 > 3 > 4

My Goal
I can write a personal narrative.

Expert Model

Features of a Personal Narrative

A personal narrative tells a story from the writer's life.

- It is usually written in the first person.

- It has a beginning, middle, and end.

- It uses words and phrases to tell events in order.

*Literature Anthology:
pages 234-237*

Analyze an Expert Model Studying "Landing on Your Feet" will help you learn more about writing a personal narrative. Reread page 235. Answer the questions below.

How does Ryan use dialogue to tell an important detail?

_____

_____

How does Ryan use describing words?

_____

_____

Plan: Brainstorm

Generate Ideas You will write a personal narrative about a time you helped others. Brainstorm words and draw pictures that tell about the times you have helped.

Quick Tip

To help you get started, think about why you helped others and how it made you feel.

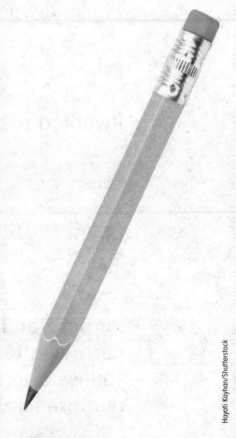

Hayati Kayhan/Shutterstock

CHECK IN 1 2 3 4

Plan: Choose Your Topic

COLLABORATE

Writing Prompt Write a personal narrative about doing something good for your school, community, or the environment. You can also write about helping friends or your family. Use your ideas from page 91. Complete these sentences to help you get started.

Quick Tip

Your audience may include your classmates or family who do not know about the events in your personal narrative. As you write, think about how to present your ideas in a clear and interesting way.

I helped when I _____

_____

I wanted to do this because _____

_____

I felt _____

_____

Purpose and Audience Authors may write personal narratives to share special experiences. Think about why you want to tell about a time you helped. Explain your purpose for writing in your writer's notebook.

CHECK IN 1 2 3 4

Ken Karp/McGraw-Hill Education

Plan: Organization

Sequence Writers often organize personal narratives with a beginning, middle, and end. Read the details in the sequence chart. **Circle** words the writer uses to help show when things take place in the different parts of the story.

 Plan In your writer's notebook, make a Sequence chart to organize the details in your personal narrative.

Beginning
One spring day, we decided to repair the playground.

↓

Middle
The next weekend, we had a flea market to raise money for the repairs.

↓

End
By summer, we repaired the playground equipment.

Draft

COLLABORATE

Focus on an Event The author of "Landing on Your Feet" tells how she helps her dad when he hurts his ankle. Reread this paragraph on page 237. Ryan focuses on taking care of Dad with details about how she helped.

> Over the weekend, Mom and I stayed home with Dad. I got fresh ice packs for his ankle, and I made him lunch and snacks. We watched movies, and I got Dad books to read. Even our kitty, Toast, helped. He lay across Dad to keep him company.

Use the paragraph as a model to write specific details about how you helped. Remember to focus on an event.

_____

_____

_____

Write a Draft Look over your Sequence chart. Use it to help you write your draft in your notebook. Remember to use words and phrases that help your readers understand the sequence of events.

Quick Tip

Think about your actions during the event you describe. Add details that will help your readers visualize, or picture, what happened during the event.

Grammar Connections

Past-tense action verbs tell about an action that has already happened. Remember to add -ed to most verbs to form the past tense.

I **helped** the adults.

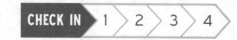
CHECK IN 1 2 3 4

Revise

Conclusion The conclusion of a personal narrative often shares how an author feels about an event. Think about what you want your readers to take away from your writing.

Reread the last paragraph of the selection on page 237. Think about how the author, Ryan, shares how she felt at the end of her story.

Explain how Ryan shows how she felt after helping.

_____

_____

_____

_____

_____

 Revise It's time to revise your draft. Make sure you write a conclusion that tells how you feel about what you did.

Revise: Peer Conferences

COLLABORATE

Review a Draft Listen carefully as a partner reads his or her work aloud. Begin by telling what you liked about the draft. Make suggestions that you think will make the writing stronger.

Partner Feedback Write one of your partner's suggestions that you will use in the revision of your narrative.

Based on my partner's feedback, I will _____

_____

_____

After you finish giving each other feedback, reflect on the peer conference. What was helpful? What might you do differently next time?

_____

_____

Revision Use the Revising Checklist to help you figure out what text you may need to move, add to, or delete. Remember to use the rubric on page 99 to help you with your revision.

Quick Tip

Use these sentence starters to discuss your partner's work.

I enjoyed this part of your draft because...

How about adding more details about...

I have a question about...

 Revising Checklist

☐ Did I write in the first person and include details?

☐ Does my personal narrative tell about an event?

☐ Did I include a beginning, middle, and end?

☐ Did I write a conclusion?

Edit and Proofread

When you **edit** and **proofread,** you look for and correct mistakes in your writing. Rereading a revised draft several times will help you catch any errors. Use the checklist below to edit your sentences.

Grammar Connections

When you write your personal narrative, make sure you use capital letters for proper nouns. Check for nouns that name specific people, places, or things.

✔ Editing Checklist

- ☐ Do all sentences begin with a capital letter and end with a punctuation mark?
- ☐ Are present-tense and past-tense forms of action verbs used correctly?
- ☐ Are all the words spelled correctly?
- ☐ Are proper nouns capitalized?

List two mistakes you found as you proofread your narrative.

1 _____

_____

2 _____

_____

Publish, Present, and Evaluate

Publishing Create a clean, neat final copy of your personal narrative. You may add illustrations or other visuals to make your published work more interesting.

Presentation Practice your presentation when you are ready to present your work. Use the Presenting Checklist to help you.

Evaluate After you publish and present your personal narrative, use the rubric on the next page to evaluate your writing.

1 What did you do successfully? _____

_____

_____

2 What needs more work? _____

_____

_____

_____

✓ Presenting Checklist

☐ Sit up or stand up straight.

☐ Look at the audience.

☐ Read with expression.

☐ Speak loudly so that everyone can hear you.

☐ Answer questions using details from your story.

4	3	2	1
• tells a lively, interesting narrative about being helpful • Includes a strong beginning, middle, and end • focuses on one event • uses words accurately to show sequence • has a strong conclusion and tells the author's feelings	• tells a narrative about being helpful • includes a beginning, middle, and end • mostly focuses on one event • uses words to show sequence • has some details about the author's feelings and a conclusion	• tries to tell a narrative about being helpful • attempts to include a beginning, middle, and an end • tries to focus on one event • uses a word or phrase to show sequence • has a detail about the author's feelings but lacks a conclusion	• does not focus on the topic • does not follow a logical sequence of events • does not focus on one event • lacks words that show sequence • does not tell about the author's feelings or have a conclusion

Turn to page 89. Fill in the bars to show what you learned.

My Goal

I can write an expository essay.

Expert Model

Features of an Expository Essay

Authors write expository essays to give information about a topic.

- An expository essay give facts and information.

- It can have text features such as photos and captions.

- It has a strong opening and a conclusion.

Literature Anthology: pages 262–265

Analyze an Expert Model Studying "Many Ways to Enjoy Music" will help you learn to write an expository essay. Reread page 265. Answer the questions below.

COLLABORATE

How does the author use language to help you understand how the special chair works?

_____

_____

_____

Word Wise

The author uses phrases such as *one way* and *another way* to help you understand that there are different ways to enjoy music.

What is the author's concluding statement?

_____

_____

_____

Plan: Brainstorm

Generate Ideas You will write an expository essay that tells about music or a musical instrument. To begin, brainstorm types of music and words related to music. Draw pictures of musical instruments. You will choose your topic from your ideas.

Quick Tip

To help you get started, think about a favorite musical instrument or a type of music you want to learn more about. You may also look through books, magazines, or websites to find pictures and words related to music.

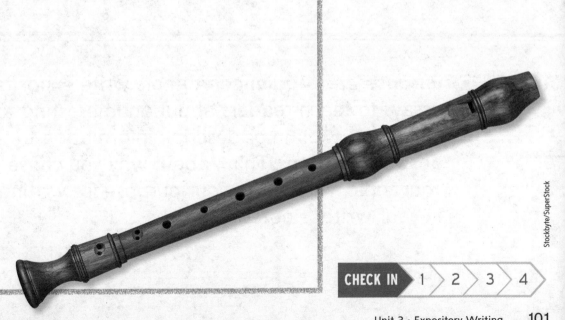

Stockbyte/SuperStock

CHECK IN 1 2 3 4

Plan: Choose Your Topic

COLLABORATE

Writing Prompt Write an expository essay that tells about a type of music or a musical instrument. Go back to the ideas you brainstormed on page 101 to choose your topic. Complete these sentences to help you get started.

Quick Tip

Your readers may include classmates or others who don't know about your topic. Think about how to make the information interesting and easy to understand.

My topic is _____

_____

This topic interests me because _____

_____

_____

Purpose and Audience Authors write expository essays to teach readers about an interesting topic. They may explain or describe information to answer questions. Think about why you chose your topic. Then write your purpose for writing in your writer's notebook.

jianying yin/E+/Getty Images

CHECK IN ⟩ 1 ⟩ 2 ⟩ 3 ⟩ 4

Plan: Research

Choose and Evaluate Sources Reliable sources have facts that can be proven to be correct. To evaluate sources of information you can use, make sure that:

- the author is an expert on your topic.

- the information is accurate and not too difficult.

Mark these types of sources as reliable or not reliable.

Sources	Reliable	Not Reliable
textbooks	✓	
blogs or social media		
encyclopedias		
education websites		

Plan Identify the one best source you will use to research your topic. Write down the source in your writer's notebook.

CHECK IN 1 2 3 4

Draft

Paragraphs A paragraph is a group of sentences that tell about one idea. The first word of a paragraph is usually indented. Reread page 264 of "Many Ways to Enjoy Music" in the **Literature Anthology**.

What idea do the details in the paragraph tell about?

_____

Now use the paragraph as a model to write a paragraph of your essay. Make sure the details tell about one idea.

_____

_____

_____

Quick Tip

Outline paragraphs for your essay. Write a sentence that tells what a paragraph will be about. Under the sentence, list details from your notes that tell about the idea.

 Write a Draft Use the information you gathered from your sources to write a draft in your writer's notebook.

Digital Tools

To learn more about creating an outline, watch "Outline to Draft." Go to **my.mheducation.com**.

CHECK IN ⟩ 1 ⟩ 2 ⟩ 3 ⟩ 4 ⟩

Revise

Strong Opening A strong opening will grab the reader's attention so that he or she wants to read more. A strong opening also states the topic of the expository essay.

Reread a student's opening paragraph below. Talk with a partner about how it grabs your attention. Write your ideas on the lines below.

COLLABORATE

> What is better than banging on the drums in the middle of a school day? Nothing, in my opinion. Music class is my favorite part of the day. We learn about instruments and make music.

_____

_____

_____

Revise It's time to revise your draft. Think about how you can write a strong opening to your essay. Make sure each paragraph has facts that tell about one idea.

Quick Tip

As you revise, think about information you researched that grabbed your attention. These facts or details about your topic can help you write a strong opening to your essay.

SolStock/E+/Getty Images

CHECK IN 1 > 2 > 3 > 4

Revise: Peer Conferences

COLLABORATE

Review a Draft Listen carefully as a partner reads his or her work aloud. Begin by telling what you like about the draft. Make suggestions that you think will make the writing stronger.

Partner Feedback Write one of your partner's suggestions that you will use in the revision of your text.

Based on my partner's feedback, I will _____

_____

_____

After you finish giving each other feedback, reflect on the peer conference. What was helpful? What might you do differently next time?

_____

_____

Revision Use the Revising Checklist to help you figure out what text you may need to move, add to, or delete. Remember to use the rubric on page 109 to help you with your revision.

Remember to use the rubric on page 109

Quick Tip

Use these sentence starters to discuss your partner's work.

Where did you find the information about...

Can you explain how...

I think that it would be clearer to say...

✓ Revising Checklist

☐ Does my essay tell about the topic?

☐ Does each paragraph tell about one idea?

☐ Does it have a strong opening?

☐ Does it have a conclusion?

☐ Are the sources clearly cited?

Edit and Proofread

When you **edit** and **proofread**, you look for and correct mistakes in your writing. Rereading a revised draft several times will help you catch any errors. Use the checklist below to edit your sentences.

Tech Tip

If you type your text, use the "Tab" key to indent each paragraph.

✓ Editing Checklist

- ☐ Do all sentences end with the correct punctuation mark?
- ☐ Does the verb agree with the subject in each sentence?
- ☐ Are the verbs used correctly in the past and future tenses?
- ☐ Is the word "have" used correctly?
- ☐ Are all of the words spelled correctly?

List two mistakes you found as you proofread your text.

1 _____

_____

2 _____

_____

Grammar Connections

As you proofread, make sure you correctly used different types of nouns in sentences. Remember, a collective noun names a group that acts as one thing.

*Our **band** practices on Monday.*

Publish, Present, and Evaluate

Publishing Create a neat, clean final copy of your expository essay. Add illustrations or a diagram to make your published work more interesting.

Presentation Practice your presentation when you are ready to present your work. Use the Presenting Checklist to help you.

Evaluate After you publish and present your essay, use the rubric on the next page to evaluate your writing.

1 What did you do successfully? _____

_____

_____

2 What needs more work? _____

_____

_____

Presenting Checklist

- ☐ Sit up or stand up straight.
- ☐ Look at different people in the audience.
- ☐ Speak slowly and clearly.
- ☐ Speak loudly so that everyone can hear you.
- ☐ Answer questions using facts from your text.

4	3	2	1
• focuses on a topic related to music • has a strong opening and a concluding statement or section • each paragraph tells about an idea • is free or almost free of errors	• focuses mostly on one topic related to music • introduces the topic in the opening and has a conclusion • in each paragraph, most details relate to one idea • has few errors	• lacks focus on a topic • does not have a strong opening and lacks a conclusion • attempts to write complete paragraphs • has errors that distract from the meaning of the essay	• does not focus on a topic • does not have an opening or a conclusion • does not organize ideas into paragraphs • has many errors that make the essay hard to understand

Turn to page 89. Fill in the bars to show what you learned.

My Goal I can read and understand science texts.

TAKE NOTES

Take notes and annotate as you read the passages "Electric Cars" and "Heating Homes."

Look for the answer to the question: *What kinds of energy do people use in their everyday lives?*

PASSAGE 1 EXPOSITORY TEXT

Electric Cars

More than 250 million cars are on the road in America! Engineers work to make better cars. They want to make cars safer. They want them to use less gas to save drivers money. Electric cars use less gas. They can reduce pollution, too.

Two Types of Electric Cars

Hybrid electric cars have a regular engine and an electric motor. The engine uses gas. The motor uses electricity from energy stored in batteries. The

The number of charging stations is increasing as more people buy electric cars.

batteries are charged by the engine. Some hybrid cars can also be plugged in to charge the batteries.

All-electric cars run on an electric motor. They are powered by electricity from batteries. The batteries recharge by plugging the car in.

Nerthuz/Alamy Stock Photo

Benefits and Problems

Electric cars use less fuel than regular cars. So it costs less to drive them. They also make less pollution. But hybrids and all-electric cars cost more money. All-electric cars drive fewer miles on a charge than regular cars drive on a tank of gas. It can take a long time to recharge the batteries.

Today, more people still drive regular cars. Do you think electric cars are a better choice for families?

Comparing Electric and Standard Cars

+ = benefit
− = problem

Electric Cars	Standard Cars
+ use less gas + cost less to drive + make less pollution	+ cost less to buy + can refill at any gas station
− cost more to buy − batteries take time to charge − not many places to charge batteries	− cost more to drive—have to buy gas − not as efficient as electric vehicles

TAKE NOTES

_____

_____

_____

_____

_____

_____

_____

_____

_____

_____

_____

_____

_____

PASSAGE **EXPOSITORY TEXT**

2

POWERING HOMES

Most homes use electricity for power. Renewable energy can make some or all of the electricity a home needs. Renewable energy can help reduce pollution.

Solar Power Solar panels can change light from the Sun into electricity. The electricity can then be used to heat and cool homes. Solar panels are usually put on the top of buildings. They only make electricity when the Sun is shining.

Wind Power Wind can be turned into electricity. A wind turbine has two or three large blades. The blades look like a propeller on an airplane. Wind turns the blades. The blades spin and produce energy. This energy is used to make electricity.

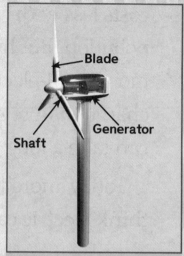

Blade

Generator

Shaft

When wind turns the blades, they turn a shaft. The shaft spins a generator to make electricity.

Dorling Kindersley/Getty Images

Geothermal Energy Geothermal energy can heat and cool homes without making electricity. Heat pumps use energy from the warmth of the earth to heat and cool homes.

Underground, the temperature of the earth stays about the same all year long. So the ground is warmer than the air in the winter and cooler than the air in the summer. Heat pumps move heat between the ground and a home. In the summer, the pump takes heat out of the air. It moves the heat through pipes into the ground, so the house gets cooler. In the winter, the pump takes heat from the ground. It moves the heat into the house, making it warm.

These sources of renewable energy help people stay comfortable. And they help Earth too!

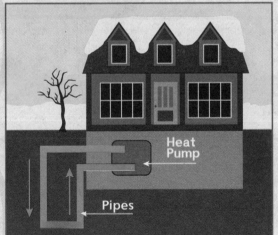

Heat pumps help move heat from the ground into a house to heat it.

TAKE NOTES

Compare the Passages

Talk About It Reread your notes from "Electric Cars" and "Powering Homes." Discuss what you learned about the energy people use in their daily lives.

Cite Text Evidence Fill in the Venn diagram with information from the passages.

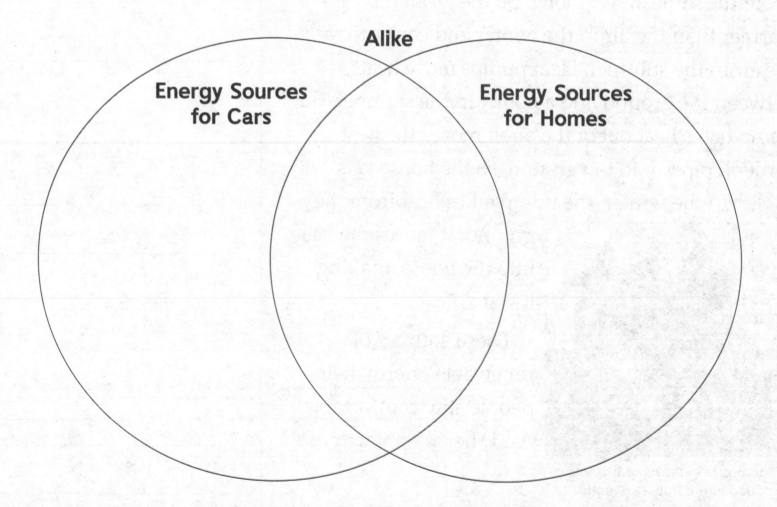

Alike

Energy Sources for Cars

Energy Sources for Homes

? What kinds of energy do people use in their everyday lives?

Talk About It Look at the Venn diagram on page 114. Talk about "Electric Cars" and "Powering Homes." Explain how people use electricity in their daily lives. Use examples from the passages.

Write People use electricity to _____

_____

_____

_____

_____

Quick Tip

Use these sentence starters to talk about the energy people use in their daily lives.

Some sources of energy are...

Electricity is used...

Renewable energy can...

💡 **Combine Information**

People use electricity every day. Electricity can come from different sources. Why is it important to know about different ways to make electricity? What choices can people make about the energy they use?

CHECK IN 1 2 3 4

Learn More About the Sun's Energy

COLLABORATE

Sunlight can be used to make electricity for homes. There are other ways people can use the energy from the Sun. Do this experiment to learn more.

1. **Gather materials.** See sidebar.

2. **Measure.** Pour 1 cup of water into each bowl. Measure and record the first temperatures in the chart below.

3. **Make a prediction.** Put Bowl 1 in a sunny place. Put Bowl 2 in a dark place. What do you think will happen to the temperature of the water in each bowl? Write your idea here.

_____

_____

4. **Record data.** Measure and record the second temperatures at the end of the day.

	1ˢᵗ temperature	2ⁿᵈ temperature
Bowl 1		
Bowl 2		

Materials

2 bowls

Measuring cup

Water

Thermometer

Mark Steinmetz/McGraw-Hill Education; Dot Box Inc./McGraw-Hill Education; Alex Cao/Digital Vision/Getty Images; Ken Cavanagh/McGraw-Hill Education

Write About Your Results

After you finish the experiment, think about the results. Write a conclusion about what happened to the water in each bowl. Explain what this tells you about energy from the Sun.

_____

_____

_____

Do the results match your prediction? Why or why not?

_____

_____

Scientists are always asking questions and doing experiments to learn more about the world. Discuss questions you have about the Sun's energy. What experiments could you do to answer these questions?

IhorL/Shutterstock

My Goal I can read and understand social studies texts.

TAKE NOTES

Take notes and annotate as you read the passages "Flying Firsts" and "Landing the Eagle."

Look for the answer to the question: *How does knowing the order of events help you understand a topic?*

PASSAGE **1**

EXPOSITORY TEXT

Flying Firsts

Birds can fly naturally. But it took people from all over the world thousands of years to make human flight possible.

Kites More than 2,000 years ago, people in China made the first objects to fly in the sky: kites! The first kites were made out of bamboo and silk. They were used to carry messages and measure distances.

Hot-Air Balloons In 1783 in Paris, France, two brothers launched the first hot-air balloon. They sent a sheep, a duck, and a rooster up in the air. The animals landed safely after a short flight. Inventors went on to make balloons that could carry people.

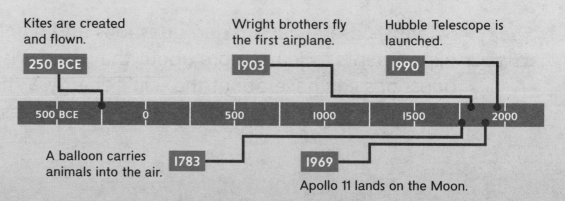

Kites are created and flown.
250 BCE

Wright brothers fly the first airplane.
1903

Hubble Telescope is launched.
1990

500 BCE | 0 | 500 | 1000 | 1500 | 2000

A balloon carries animals into the air.
1783

1969

Apollo 11 lands on the Moon.

D. Hurst/Alamy Stock Photo

The Wright brothers

Airplanes More than one century later, the first airplane took off in Kitty Hawk, North Carolina. It was made of wood and looked like a kind of kite, the box kite! It only flew for a few seconds. But it changed the world.

Spaceships In the 20th century, the United States and Russia raced to fly into space. The Russians sent the first person into space. The Americans were the first to land on the Moon in 1969. Since then, humans have launched a space station, space shuttles, rockets, and telescopes. Where do you think we will fly to next?

Apollo 11

(t) Wright Brothers Negatives, Library of Congress, LC-DIG-ppprs-00626; (b) NASA

TAKE NOTES

TAKE NOTES

PASSAGE **2**

EXPOSITORY TEXT

LANDING THE EAGLE

APOLLO 11

More than five decades ago, astronaut Neil Armstrong was sitting in a tiny spaceship called *Eagle*. He was flying toward the Moon. Neil watched as *Eagle* got closer to the Moon. Suddenly, he saw a big problem ahead. *Eagle's* landing computers were heading toward a field of giant rocks the size of cars! He knew that this landing spot was unsafe. The rocks could tip over *Eagle*. That would damage his ship. He would be unable to leave the Moon forever!

Then, Neil made an important decision. He turned off the computers. He would steer the ship himself. He was worried about landing the ship safely. The ship was also almost out of fuel. Neil had to find a place to land soon!

Neil guided *Eagle* carefully past the giant rocks. He saw a wide, flat field up ahead.

NASA

"That is the place!" he thought. Slowly, he lowered *Eagle* onto the field. But his rocket boosters blew a big cloud of dust into the air. Neil was blinded as he guided *Eagle* down.

Finally, *Eagle's* small feet thumped onto the Moon. Neil breathed a sigh of relief. Then he clicked his radio and sent a happy message back home.

"Houston . . . The Eagle has landed."

Neil Armstrong was the first person to walk on the Moon. He placed a flag on the Moon to show that America's astronauts reached it first.

TAKE NOTES

Compare the Passages

Talk About It Reread your notes from "Flying Firsts" and "Landing the Eagle." Discuss how the authors use words and dates to tell when events took place. How do they help you understand the sequence of the events?

Cite Text Evidence Fill in the chart with words or dates from the passages that tell the sequence of events.

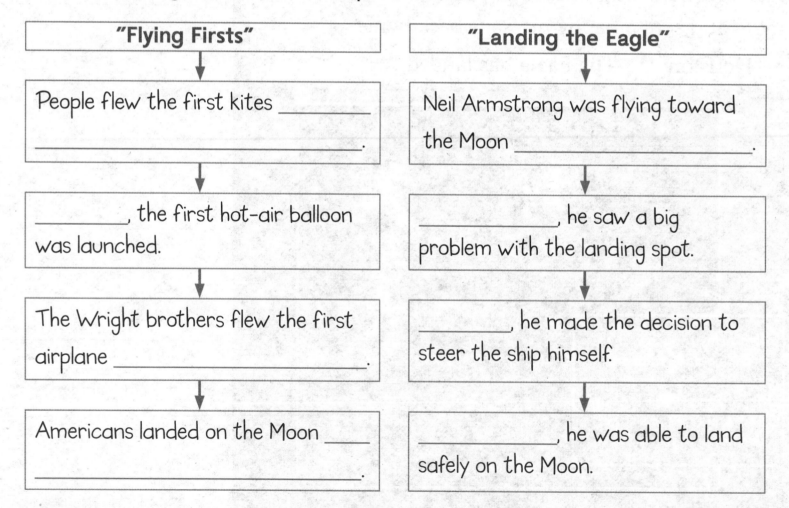

"Flying Firsts"	"Landing the Eagle"
People flew the first kites _____ _____.	Neil Armstrong was flying toward the Moon _____.
_____, the first hot-air balloon was launched.	_____, he saw a big problem with the landing spot.
The Wright brothers flew the first airplane _____.	_____, he made the decision to steer the ship himself.
Americans landed on the Moon _____ _____.	_____, he was able to land safely on the Moon.

? **How does knowing the order of events help you understand a topic?**

Talk About It Look at the graphic organizer on page 122. Talk about "Flying Firsts" and "Landing the Eagle." Why do the authors use time words and sequence words to help you understand the topics?

Write "Flying Firsts" helps me understand _____

_____

_____

_____

I understand the events in "Landing the Eagle" because

_____

_____

_____

Quick Tip

Use these sentence starters to talk about how the words the authors use help you understand the events.

Time words tell...

Sequence words show...

I understand the order of events because...

Combine Information

How do words and dates help you understand topics in social studies? Why is it important to know the order in which things happened? Why is it important to know how long ago something happened?

CHECK IN 1 2 3 4

Create a Timeline

Choose one of the people shown below. Use print or online sources to create a timeline. Show four or more key events in the life of the person you choose.

Orville Wright	Amelia Earhart
Ronald McNair	Sally Ride

- Mark the years in decades.

- Write the person's date of birth on the timeline.

- Use short phrases or sentences to describe at least four important events or accomplishments in the person's life.

- Include a photo or drawing with the timeline.

Write a sentence that summarizes the information on your timeline.

_____

_____

Share the information on your timeline with a partner. Discuss the events you included. Finally, talk about how timelines can help readers understand a person's life.

Quick Tip

In your timeline, show the events in time order. Begin with the person's date of birth. If an important event happened between two decades, mark the point between the decades when it occurred.

Ronald McNair was an American physicist and astronaut.

Reflect on Your Learning

Talk About It Reflect on what you learned in this unit. Then talk with a partner about how you did.

I am really proud of how I can _____

_____

_____

_____

_____

Something I need to work more on is _____

_____

_____

_____

Share a goal you have with a partner.

My Goal Set a goal for Unit 4. In your reader's notebook, write about what you can do to get there.